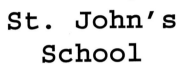

St. John's School

Given by
Drs. Roselyn & Charles Epps

In honor of
Campbell Charles Epps '23

Book Fair 2011

Spiders

Debbie and Brendan Gallagher

Marshall Cavendish
Benchmark
New York

Contents

When a word is printed in **bold**, you can look up its meaning in the Glossary on page 31.

Mighty Minibeasts

Minibeasts are small animals, such as flies and spiders. Although they are small, minibeasts are a mighty collection of animals. They belong to three animal groups: arthropods, molluscs, or annelids.

	Animal Group		
	Arthropods	**Molluscs**	**Annelids**
Main Feature	Arthropods have an outer skeleton and a body that is divided into sections.	Most molluscs have a soft body that is not divided into sections.	Annelids have a soft body made up of many sections.
Examples of Minibeasts	Insects, such as ants, beetles, cockroaches, and wasps **Arachnids**, such as spiders and scorpions Centipedes and millipedes	Snails and slugs	Earthworms Leeches

More than three-quarters of all animals are minibeasts!

Spiders

Spiders are minibeasts. They belong to the arthropod group of animals. This means that they have an outer skeleton and a body that is divided into sections. Spiders are a type of arachnid.

Spiders are closely related to scorpions.

What Do Spiders Look Like?

Spiders have two main body parts. The back part is called the **abdomen**. The front part is both the head and the **thorax**. Spiders have eight legs joined to the thorax.

How can I tell if it is a spider? Spiders have eight legs, create silk, and are often seen living on webs.

Spiders have spinnerets at the back of their abdomen, used for spinning webs.

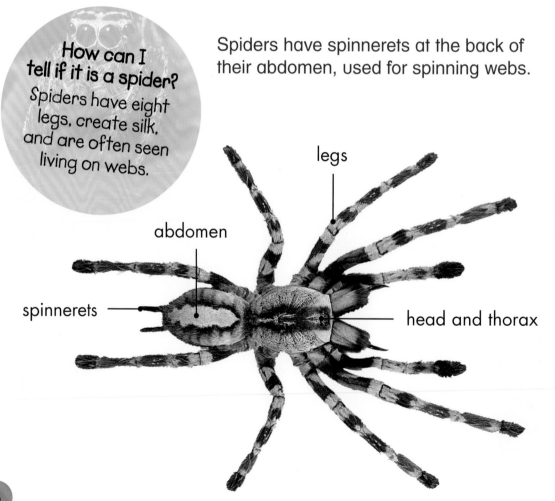

legs

abdomen

spinnerets

head and thorax

Spiders have eight eyes on the front of their head. They have two small feelers, called palps, and two fangs to attack their **prey**.

Spiders use their unique features to sense the world around them.

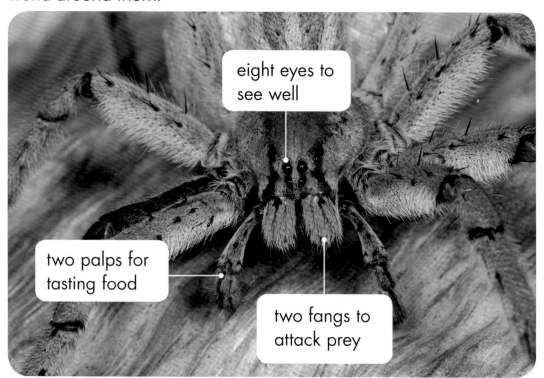

eight eyes to see well

two palps for tasting food

two fangs to attack prey

Different Types of Spiders

There are more than 40,000 different **species** of spiders. The largest spiders have a body 7 inches (18 centimeters) long. The smallest spiders have a body less than ¹⁄₂₄ inch (1 millimeter) long.

¹⁄₂₄ inch (1 millimeter)

This crab spider is one of the world's smallest spiders

7 inches (18 centimeters)

Goliath tarantulas are the largest spiders in the world.

Spiders come in different shapes and colors. Most spiders are brown or black, but others can be green, gray, or other colors. Some spiders have patterns on their bodies.

This happy-face spider is green with a red pattern that looks like a smile.

This wolf spider has a gray body with dark and light areas.

Where in the World Are Spiders Found?

Spiders can be found on every continent except Antarctica. They can also be found on most islands.

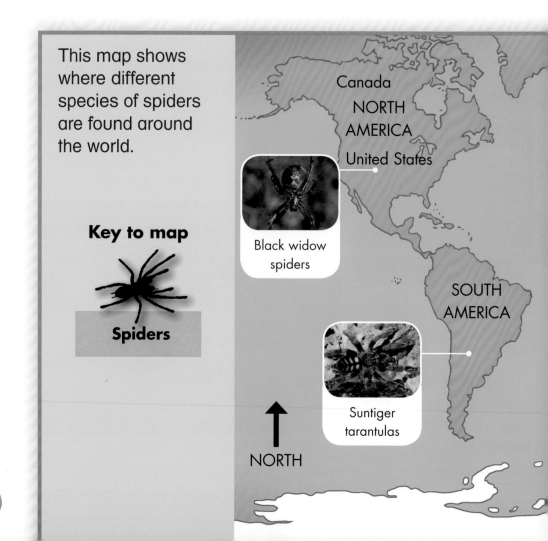

This map shows where different species of spiders are found around the world.

Key to map

Spiders

Canada

NORTH AMERICA

United States

Black widow spiders

SOUTH AMERICA

Suntiger tarantulas

NORTH

Spiders are not found in places that are extremely cold, such as high mountain tops.

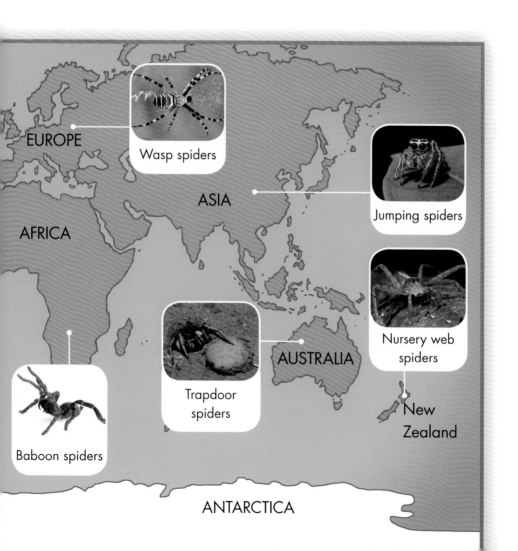

EUROPE

Wasp spiders

ASIA

Jumping spiders

AFRICA

Nursery web spiders

Trapdoor spiders

AUSTRALIA

New Zealand

Baboon spiders

ANTARCTICA

Habitats of Spiders

Spiders can live in nearly all **habitats**, including deserts, grasslands, and forests. Some spiders live in caves, while others can even live in water.

Mouse spiders live in dry, grassy areas.

Some spiders live around humans, in farms, towns, and cities. They make their homes in the corners of sheds or houses.

Some house spiders live in window frames.

Life Cycles of Spiders

A life cycle diagram shows the stages of a spider's life, from newborn to adult.

1. A male spider and a female spider **mate**. The female lays her eggs inside an egg sac made from silk.

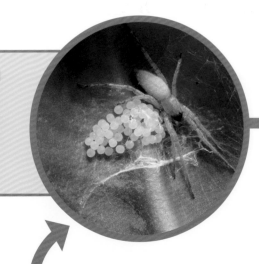

4. As the spiderlings grow, they grow a new outer layer of skin. When they become adult spiders, they continue molting.

molted skin

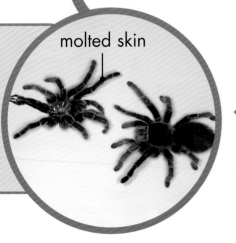

Some species of spiders lay as many as six hundred eggs in one egg sac. Other species will lay only four eggs in one egg sac.

2. Young spiders, called spiderlings, hatch from the eggs. Spiderlings stay near the egg sac for a few days.

3. Before leaving the egg sac, the spiderlings get rid of their outer layer of skin. This is called molting. After molting, they leave the egg sac.

How Do Spiders Live?

Most spiders live on their own. Female spiders often stay with their spiderlings until they can look after themselves.

This female wolf spider is carrying her spiderlings on her back while she hunts for food.

spiderlings

Some species of spiders live in groups. They live together in a large web and help each other catch large insects. Any food that the spiders catch is shared.

These spiders are working together to catch a bullet ant.

bullet ant

Spider Homes

Spiders make homes in webs or **burrows**. Webs and burrows are made in places where spiders can catch food. Some spiders spin webs in places such as trees.

Many spiders make a home by spinning a web.

Some spiders make their homes in burrows in the ground. The trapdoor spider lives in a burrow hidden by a covering. It waits in hiding for prey to come along.

This trapdoor spider has come out of its burrow to catch a cockroach.

burrow

Spider Food

Spiders eat insects, such as flies. Some spiders eat other spiders. Water spiders eat tadpoles and even small fish.

Foods That Spiders Eat

Insects, such as flies	
Other spiders	
Tadpoles and small fish	

Spiders use their fangs to inject **venom** into their prey. The venom stops the prey from moving. It also turns the prey's insides to liquid, which the spider can then suck out.

fangs

Wolf spiders use their fangs to feed on prey such as blowflies.

Why Do Spiders Spin Webs?

Spiders spin webs to make a home and to catch their prey. Spiders create silk inside their bodies, then use their spinnerets to weave the silk into webs.

Some parts of an argiope spider's web are sticky for catching prey.

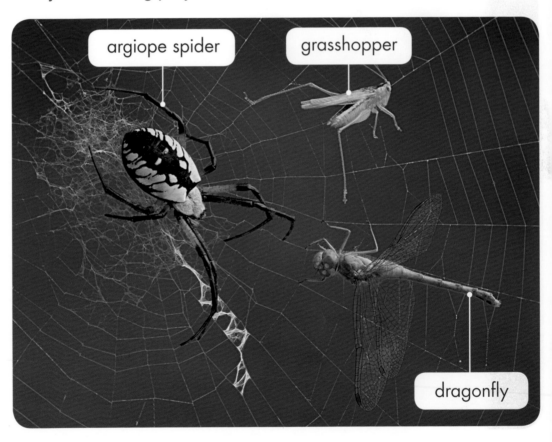

argiope spider

grasshopper

dragonfly

Different spiders can create different webs. Orb-weaving spiders weave a silk frame with sticky silk on top. Net-casting spiders weave a small net that they hold, ready to catch prey.

This net-casting spider is holding its web in its front legs, ready to catch insects.

Threats to the Survival of Spiders

Spiders are threatened by other animals. Many different **predators** feed on spiders and their eggs. These predators include:

- insects, such as mantises, wasps, and flies
- birds, such as starlings
- **reptiles**, such as lizards
- other spiders.

spider

This starling is feeding a spider to its young.

The survival of spiders is also threatened by human activities. Humans can destroy spider habitats when they build towns, farms, and roads.

The great raft spider is a threatened species because its marshland habitat is being destroyed.

Spiders and the Environment

Spiders are an important part of the **environment** they live in. Spiders feed on other animals, and many animals feed on them. This is shown in a food web.

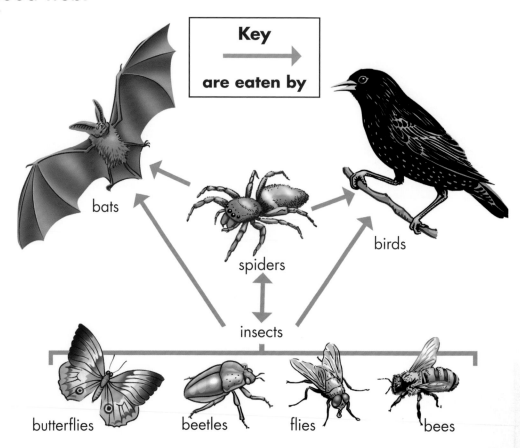

Key

are eaten by

bats

spiders

birds

insects

butterflies   beetles   flies   bees

This food web shows what spiders eat and what eats them.

Spiders hunt insects such as houseflies and mosquitoes. This reduces the number of these insects so there are not too many.

Lynx spiders feed on mosquitoes.

lynx spider

mosquito

Dangerous Spiders

Some spiders are dangerous, with sharp fangs that they use to inject venom. This venom stuns or kills their prey, and can be used to fight off predators.

Spiders inject venom into their prey using hollow fangs.

fangs

If spiders feel threatened, they may bite. However, only a few types of spiders are dangerous to people. A medicine called antivenom is used to treat spider bites.

The venom of the red-back spider and the black widow spider is dangerous to people.

red-back spider

black widow spider

Tips for Watching Spiders

These tips will help you to watch spiders:

- Look for spider webs around your house, such as in the corners of rooms.
- Check inside your shed or garage, where spiders are likely to hide.
- Use a spray bottle of water to lightly spray a web to see its shape.
- Sometimes a spider will come out of hiding if you gently touch its web with a leaf.

Look but do not touch! Watch spiders without touching them to see where they go and what they do.

You can get a good view of a spider using a magnifying glass.

Glossary

abdomen   The end section of an insect's body.

arachnids   Eight-legged animals, such as spiders, that are part of the arthropod group.

burrows   Holes in the ground made by animals as homes or places to rest.

environment   The air, water, and land that surround us.

habitats   Areas in which animals are naturally found.

mate   Join together to produce young.

predators   Animals that hunt other animals for food.

prey   Animals that are eaten by other animals as food.

reptiles   A group of animals with dry, scaly skin.

species   Groups of animals or plants that have similar features.

thorax   The part of the body between the head and abdomen.

venom   Poison.

Index